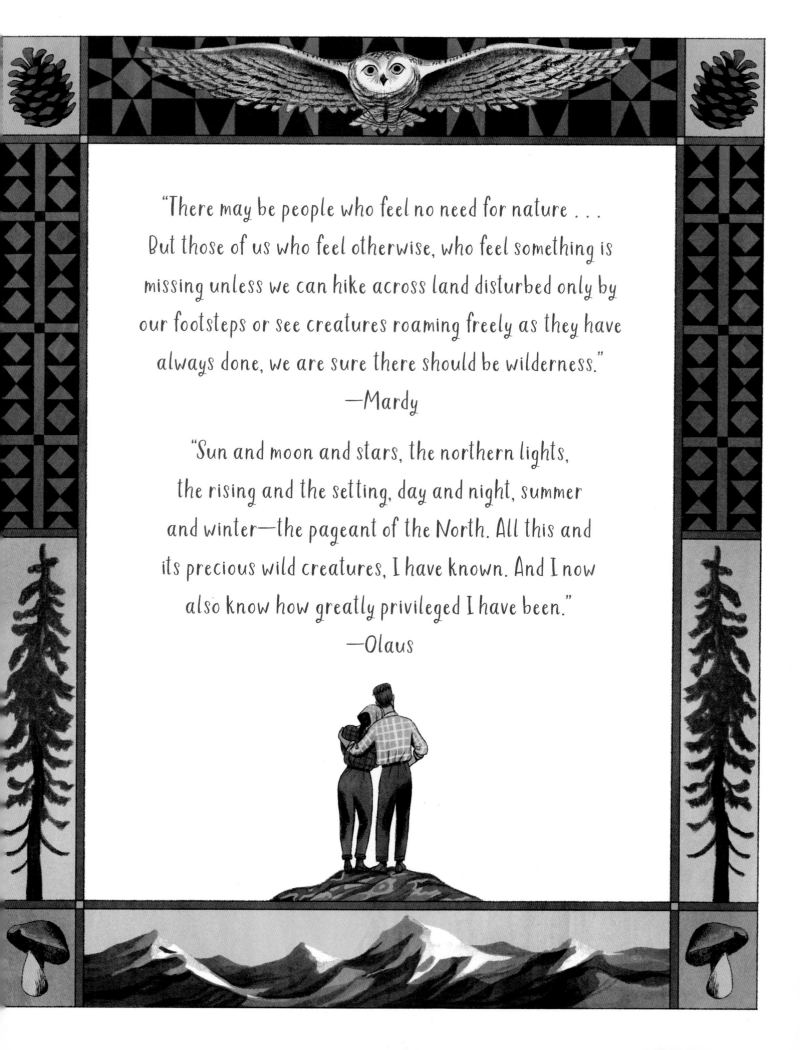

"There may be people who feel no need for nature . . .
But those of us who feel otherwise, who feel something is
missing unless we can hike across land disturbed only by
our footsteps or see creatures roaming freely as they have
always done, we are sure there should be wilderness."
—Mardy

"Sun and moon and stars, the northern lights,
the rising and the setting, day and night, summer
and winter—the pageant of the North. All this and
its precious wild creatures, I have known. And I now
also know how greatly privileged I have been."
—Olaus

For the next generation of conservationists, drawing inspiration
from the past while forging new trails into the future.
—Evan

In memory of my grandfather, Victor,
whose spirit of adventure and love of the wild was passed on to me.
—Anna

## SLEEPING BEAR PRESS™
2395 South Huron Parkway, Suite 200, Ann Arbor, MI 48104
www.sleepingbearpress.com © Sleeping Bear Press

Printed and bound in China
10 9 8 7 6 5 4 3 2 1

Library of Congress Cataloging-in-Publication Data
Names: Griffith, Evan, author. | Bron, Anna, 1989- illustrator. | Title: Wild at heart : the story of Olaus and Mardy
Murie, defenders of nature / by Evan Griffith ; and illustrated by  Anna Bron. | Other titles: Story of Olaus and Mardy
Murie, defenders of nature | Description: Ann Arbor, MI : Sleeping Bear Press, [2024] | Audience: Ages 6-10 | Summary: "In the 1900s,
Mardy and Olaus Murie set out on an Arctic adventure, studying the land and animals. They learned from Indigenous communities the
interconnectedness of life and understood that humans were threatening nature. So they fought to protect the Arctic-lobbying for what
became the Arctic National Wildlife Refuge"-- Provided by publisher. | Identifiers: LCCN 2024007520 | ISBN 9781534112919 (hardcover)
| Subjects: LCSH: Murie, Olaus J. (Olaus Johan), 1889-1963. | Murie, Olaus J. (Olaus Johan), 1889-1963--Travel. | Murie, Margaret E.
| Murie, Margaret E.--Travel. | Conservationists--Alaska--Biography. | Alaska--Description and travel. | Wilderness areas--Alaska.
| Indians of North America--Alaska. | Arctic National Wildlife Refuge (Alaska)--History. | Classification: LCC QH105.A4 M874 2024 |
DDC 508.798--dc23/eng/20240216 | LC record available at https://lccn.loc.gov/2024007520

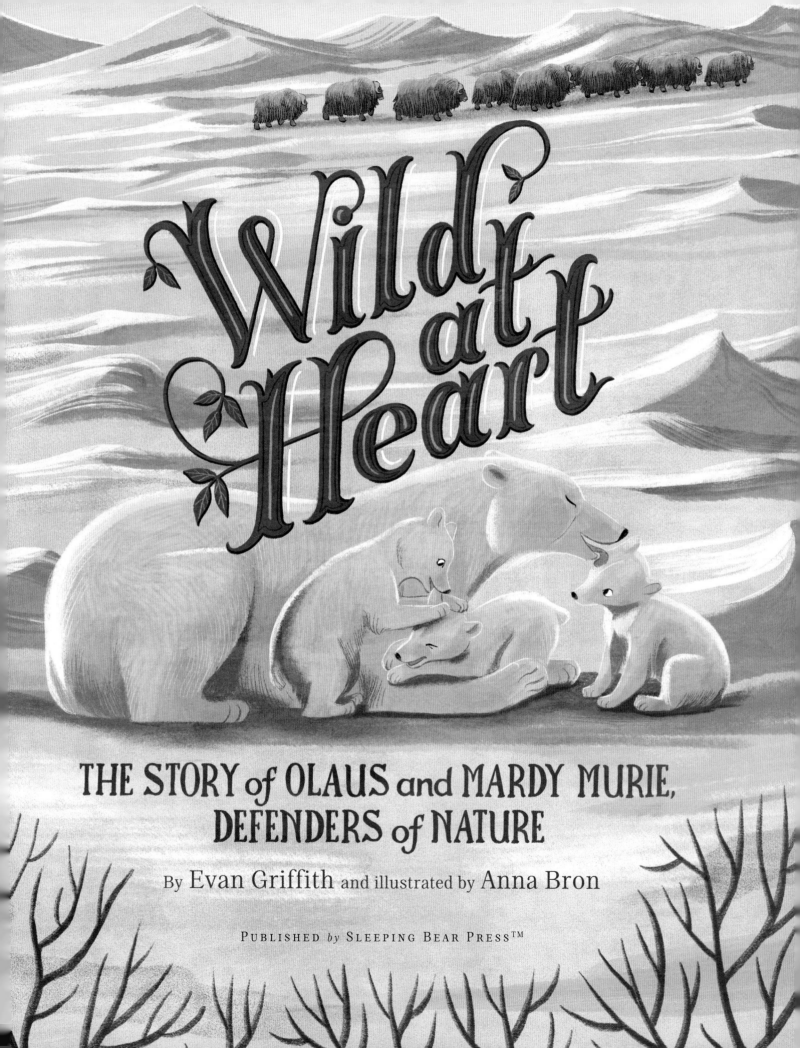

# Wild at Heart

## THE STORY of OLAUS and MARDY MURIE, DEFENDERS of NATURE

By Evan Griffith and illustrated by Anna Bron

PUBLISHED *by* SLEEPING BEAR PRESS™

Deep in the woods of Minnesota, a boy named Olaus roamed the banks of a river near his home. Sometimes, he played and laughed. Other times, he sat perfectly still—watching, listening, feeling. In quiet moments, he drew and painted the world around him.

Thousands of miles away, in snowy Alaska, a girl named Mardy sought adventure in the wilderness surrounding her tiny town. With flushed cheeks and bright eyes, she explored forests thick with spruce and willow trees and rode sleds through a frozen world of misty mountain peaks.

As Olaus grew up, he continued
to watch, listen, feel.

He became a biologist and traveled to Canada
to study the birds that live there.

As Mardy grew up, she continued to explore the Alaskan wilds. She spent summers by the sea, hiking past cascading glaciers and through marshy bogs, across fields of dazzling Arctic flowers.

Olaus and Mardy both fell in love with the natural world—with land that is great and wild and free. And when Olaus's work brought him to Mardy's town in Alaska . . .

. . . they fell in love with each other, too.

In a tiny log church lit by flickering candles and filled with wildflowers, they said their vows.

Some couples settle down after they get married.
Not Mardy and Olaus. As the sun rose on a new day
and the Alaskan sky shimmered pink and gold,
they set off for a life of science—and adventure.

As part of Olaus's work, he and Mardy crossed countless miles of Arctic wilderness to study animals. They hiked until their bones ached,

canoed down churning river rapids,

and rode dogsleds across the brilliant white snow, so fast it felt like flying. It was exhilarating—but dangerous, too.

They endured bitter cold.

Fierce blizzards.

Ice that could BOOM and CRACK
beneath their feet at any moment!

They even came face-to-face
with the great predators of the Arctic—
grizzly bears and wolves.

But Olaus and Mardy didn't face the Arctic alone.

In their travels, they met Native people from different tribes who offered food and shelter, led them through treacherous parts of the Arctic, and taught them about the animals that live there.

Along the way, Olaus and Mardy saw how the Native communities they visited lived in harmony with the natural world by respecting the land and the animals.

With the help of Native guides, Olaus and Mardy found many animals to study, from wild reindeer to geese and Arctic mice.

They filled notebooks with data and observations so they could share what they learned with the world.

It wasn't all work, though.

It was *fun.*

In fields of squishy moss, Mardy and Olaus took turns falling backward and letting the Earth catch them.

When they heard the hooting of great horned owls, they hooted back.

During long, dark winter nights, they sang and danced the cold away,
holding their arms over their heads and pretending to be reindeer.

And sometimes,
when they looked up at the night sky . . .

. . . they saw a kaleidoscope of shifting, swirling colors.

Inspired by the beauty of the Arctic and their time among Native tribes, Olaus and Mardy studied nature not just with their minds but with their hearts.

This helped them see the
bigger ideas beyond the facts.

They saw how everything in nature is connected,
from the tiniest blade of grass to the biggest grizzly.

They saw how it all comes together
to form the great chain of life.

They saw that humans are a part of this chain, too—
not masters of the Earth, but one type of animal among many.

They saw that all animals, including humans, need land
that is great and wild and free in order to live happily.

But they also saw that nature was threatened.

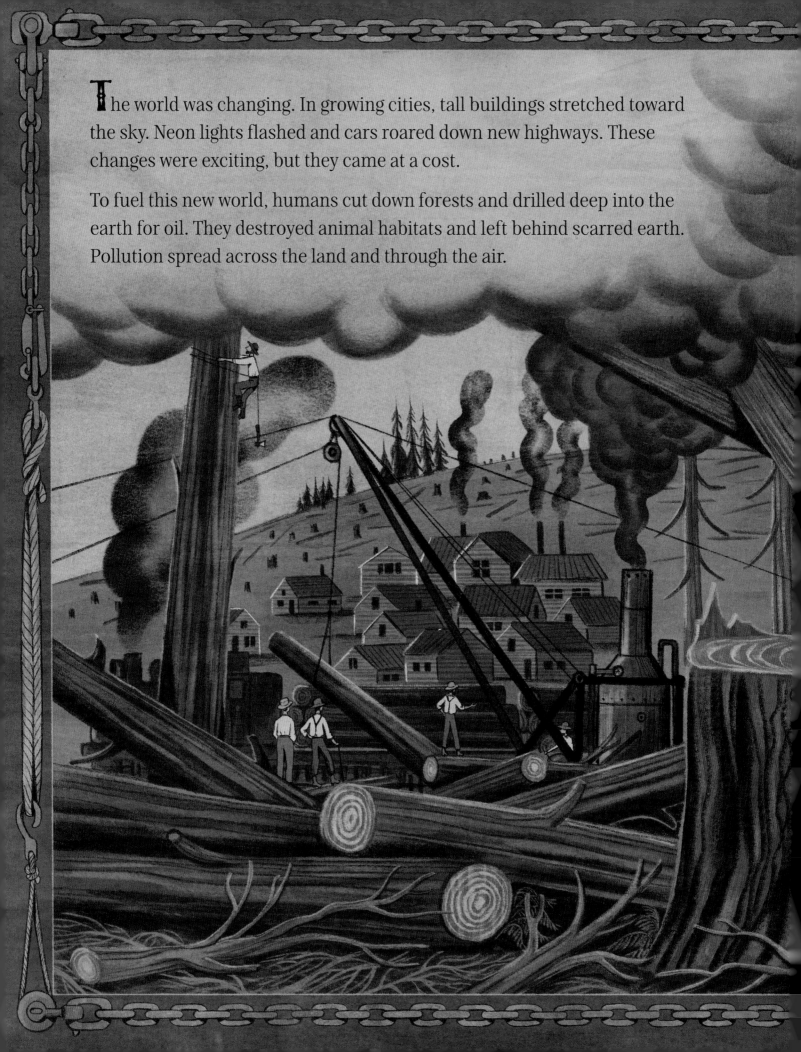

The world was changing. In growing cities, tall buildings stretched toward the sky. Neon lights flashed and cars roared down new highways. These changes were exciting, but they came at a cost.

To fuel this new world, humans cut down forests and drilled deep into the earth for oil. They destroyed animal habitats and left behind scarred earth. Pollution spread across the land and through the air.

Olaus and Mardy knew that if humans kept taking and taking, one day all of Earth's resources would be used up. What would become of the Minnesota woods Olaus had once painted? The Alaskan wilds that Mardy once explored? The lands that Native tribes had tended for so many generations?

It was time for a change, Mardy and Olaus decided. They wouldn't just study nature. They would fight for its survival by becoming conservationists, people who protect land and animals. It was a task for their minds *and* their hearts.

But where would they start?

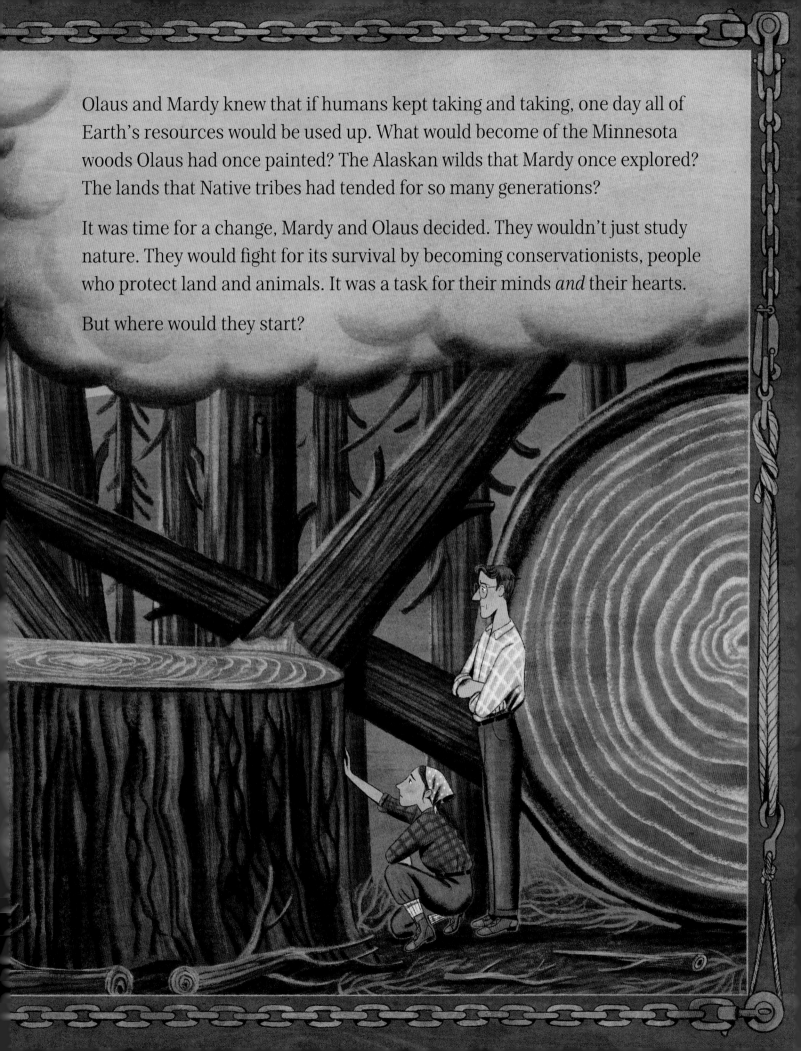

It began with a radical idea: What if large sections of nature could be set aside and protected from development, creating a refuge for all the animals and plants that live there?

At the time, most national parks were made for humans to visit. This often meant changing the environment by adding buildings and roads and removing animals that people thought were "bad," like wolves and coyotes.

But Olaus and Mardy dreamed of refuges created not for human visitors but for nature itself—areas of wilderness where the great chain of life could be unbroken, now and forever.

To make their dream a reality, they needed allies.

Olaus and Mardy traveled across the country and the world, speaking out about the need to set aside wild places—and they focused on the Arctic, the place they loved most of all.

Some people thought that scientists shouldn't be emotional—only logical. They should deal with facts, never with feelings. But Mardy and Olaus spoke with facts *and* feelings. They wove science with story, data with passion.

"I am here before you today, gentlemen, as an emotional woman . . . to tell you why . . . these areas should in all their innocence and beauty be cherished."

They didn't just ask people to set aside land. They asked people to care—
to see that nature and animals are beautiful and deserve protection.

It was a challenge. A call to action.

Not everyone liked it.

"What if such environment entirely disappears from the earth? What if a generation comes along that . . . no longer experiences the yearnings for wild country, for deep primeval forests, wilderness canoe country, high mountains, the wide expanse of desert?"

Some people didn't care about hurting the environment as long as they were making money. Protected land would just get in the way of development, they said. They accused conservationists like Olaus and Mardy of making "pretty speeches" but not being "practical." When Olaus and Mardy fought for laws to protect nature, politicians and miners fought back.

It could be discouraging, but Olaus and Mardy never quit.
They worked tirelessly—

giving speeches,

writing books and letters,

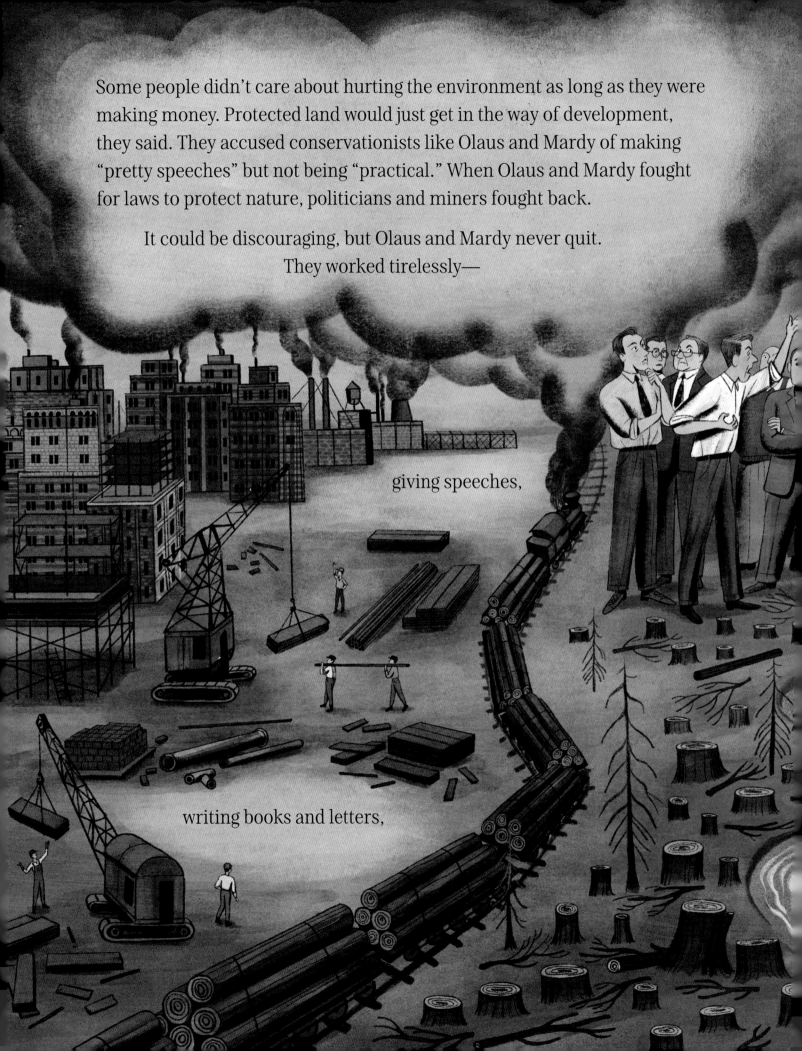

testifying before the United States Congress,

and returning to the Arctic to scout land for a wildlife refuge.

One day, their work paid off.

When Mardy received the telegram at the post office, she ran all the way home to tell Olaus the news. The United States government had decided to create the Arctic National Wildlife Refuge—over eight million acres of protected land.

Mardy and Olaus threw their arms around each other and cried tears of joy. The caribou, the wolves, the grizzlies —they all now had a safe place to live. One corner of the world would remain great and wild and free.

The victory only inspired Mardy and Olaus to keep going.

They fought for the creation of more parks and refuges. They led influential conservation societies. They persuaded the government to pass the Wilderness Act, which set aside millions of acres of wild land—not just in Alaska but all throughout the United States.

Speech by speech, letter by letter, they became voices for the wilderness and leaders of the conservation movement, guided by their minds and their hearts.

When they weren't traveling, Olaus and Mardy received visitors from all across the country at their cabin in Wyoming. Lawmakers, young scientists, students—they all came to meet the couple who had journeyed across the Arctic and then fought to protect it. They came to hear stories of danger and joy in the North. Stories of love, too—Olaus and Mardy's love for each other and their love for the wild.

These visitors were inspired. They became the next generation of conservationists, carrying on the legacy of Olaus and Mardy.

A legacy of breathless adventure.

A legacy of caring deeply for nature.

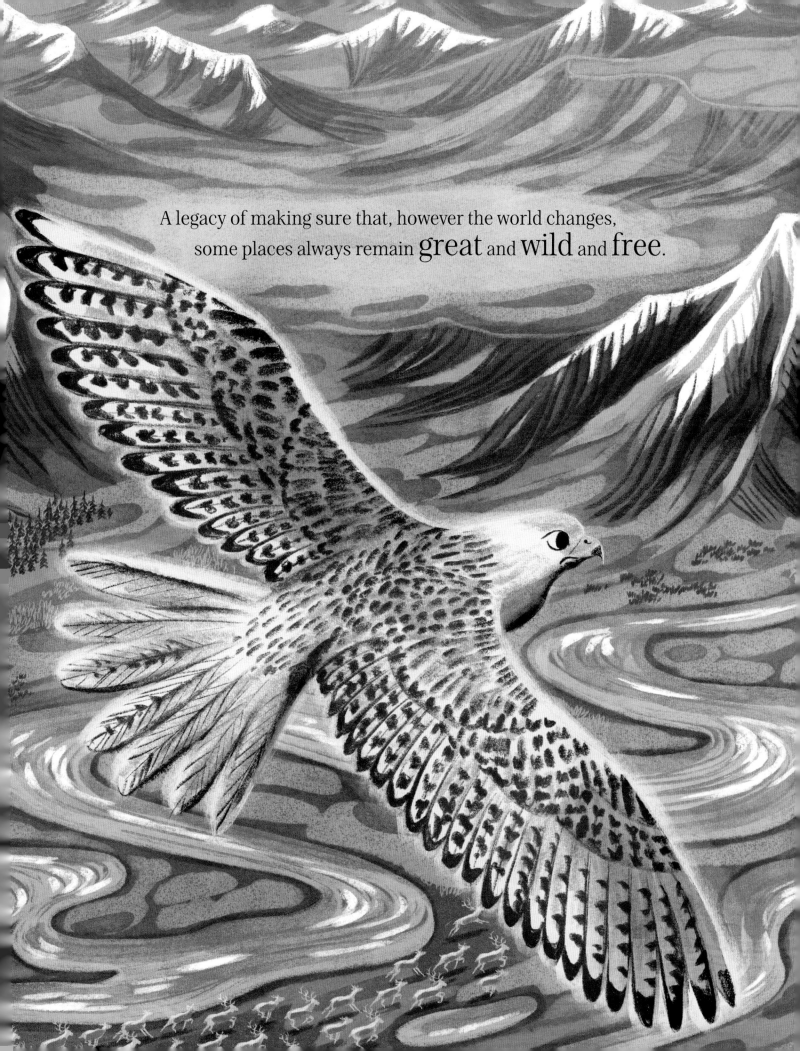

A legacy of making sure that, however the world changes,
some places always remain great and wild and free.

# Olaus Murie

Olaus Murie was born in Moorhead, Minnesota, in 1889. He developed an early love for nature by exploring the woods along the banks of the Red River near his home. He and his younger brother, Adolph, practiced their wilderness survival skills there—once, they even built their own canoe!

Olaus sketching on the deck of a ship.

Olaus studied animal biology in college. One of his early jobs was collecting animal specimens in Canada for a natural history museum. Later, the U.S. government hired Olaus to study caribou in Alaska. It was during this time that he met and fell in love with Mardy. After they married in 1924, Mardy joined Olaus on his scientific adventures in Alaska and around the world, from New Zealand to Norway. In 1927, they moved to Jackson Hole, Wyoming, where they lived for the rest of their lives when they weren't traveling.

As a scientist, Olaus developed beliefs about nature that were revolutionary at the time. While many people hated predator animals like wolves and wanted to get rid of them, Olaus defended predators, explaining that they played an important role in balancing ecosystems. He argued that the biggest threat facing animals like caribou wasn't predators but human activity, from overhunting to pollution and oil drilling. He also recognized that humans aren't separate from the animal kingdom but a part of it, sharing many traits with other species.

In 1946, these beliefs led Olaus to leave his U.S. government job and devote the rest of his life to

Mardy and Olaus near their home in Jackson Hole, Wyoming, 1953.

conservation. Along with Mardy, he became a fierce advocate for the need to preserve land in order to protect it from industrial development. Together, they influenced the creation of many parks and refuges, including the Arctic National Wildlife Refuge, established in 1960. Olaus spent the final years of his life pushing for the Wilderness Act, which would set aside over nine million acres of protected lands in the United States. The bill passed in 1964, one year after Olaus's death.

With his spirit of curiosity and gentle manner, Olaus inspired many others to follow in his footsteps, especially the young scientists who assisted him on his expeditions. His work lives on in the many books he wrote, including his memoir, *Journeys to the Far North*, as well as his illustrations. When Olaus was a child, a teacher told him to never stop drawing. He took the advice to heart. He always carried sketching paper in the back of his field notebook and often paused to draw the natural world. He believed that in order to fight for nature, we have to feel passionately about it. His drawings capture his feelings.

# Margaret "Mardy" Murie

Margaret "Mardy" Thomas was born in Seattle in 1902. At age nine, she moved with her mother to Fairbanks, Alaska, to live with her stepfather. Life there wasn't easy—Fairbanks was a tiny and isolated gold rush town and the winters were bitterly cold. But for young Mardy, Alaska was a wonderland of beautiful forests and wild rivers. Her love for nature deepened during the summers she spent at Prince William Sound among glaciers, puffins, and humpback whales.

Mardy sawing wood at camp.

Shortly after becoming the first woman to graduate from the University of Alaska, Mardy married Olaus and joined him on his scientific adventures. She assisted him with his research by recording data about animals and kept her own detailed journals about their travels.

Like Olaus, Mardy's interests shifted towards conservation work later in her life. She believed that nature had value beyond what it could offer humans and that it deserved to be protected for its own sake. She fought alongside Olaus for the creation of the Arctic National Wildlife Refuge and the passage of the Wilderness Act.

After Olaus's death in 1963, Mardy took center stage, traveling around the country to give speeches, survey land for new parks, and testify before Congress on behalf of wilderness. She protested the construction of harmful oil pipelines and **persuaded the government to add a massive expansion to the Arctic National Wildlife Refuge.** Believing strongly in the need to pass on a love of nature to the next generation, she mentored young environmentalists and helped open the Teton Science Schools, an institution devoted to environmental studies.

Olaus and Mardy dressed for Arctic adventures.

Mardy had the chance to meet multiple U.S. presidents during her lifetime. In 1964, she stood by the side of President Lyndon B. Johnson as he signed

Mardy (left) stands by President Johnson as he signs the Wilderness Act, 1964.

the Wilderness Act. In 1998, President Bill Clinton awarded her the Presidential Medal of Freedom in honor of her decades of service to nature. The story goes that when President Clinton placed the medal around her neck, she whispered in his ear, "We still have work to do."

# A Note on the Study of Historical Figures ⫷⫷

One of the challenging things about studying historical figures—especially those we admire—is learning about choices they made that we don't support, or finding contradictions in their values.

Olaus's written accounts of his Arctic travels indicate respect for the cultures and customs of the Native communities he visited. Late in the process of creating this book, though, I learned that graduate students had recently discovered ancestral remains of Native Alaskans in storage at the Murie Museum, a facility in Wyoming that houses Olaus's scientific and anthropological collections (*anthropologists* study the evolution of human beings and their cultures). Evidence suggests Olaus took these remains from a cave in Alaska during his travels. The collection of ancestral remains and funerary objects for study was a common anthropological practice at the time—but a deeply disrespectful one.

Immediately after this discovery in 2021, Teton Science Schools—the organization that operates the Murie Museum—began a formal repatriation process (*repatriation* means the return of displaced people, objects, or resources to their place of origin). The remains were returned to Alaska, and at this time of writing, they are being held at an Alaskan university museum. They are available for repatriation requests, meaning Native communities with cultural and ancestral ties to these remains may claim them. This is part of a much larger repatriation movement occurring around the world.

We might also find contradictions in Olaus's relationship to animals, which shifted throughout his life. During his early career as a wildlife biologist, part of his job was to hunt animals and send the specimens he collected to natural history museums. This, too, was a common practice at the time. Museum displays are how many people learned—and continue to learn—about animals.

As the years passed, Olaus grew less comfortable with hunting. He was fond of animals and, by all accounts, gentle by nature. When he saw a winter storm brewing, for instance, he worried about how many birds might perish in the storm. Once, Olaus and Mardy were swarmed by mosquitos in the Arctic and Olaus refused to swat a single one. When he became a conservationist, Olaus left specimen collection behind and focused on the preservation of animals and habitats. By advocating for wildlife refuges, Olaus and Mardy helped save many animal lives and protect species from extinction.

Just like each of us, historical figures were complicated and flawed. As we study history, part of our task is to acknowledge these complications. We can celebrate and draw inspiration from the wonderful things that historical people accomplished while also identifying what we would like to do differently now and in the future. We can begin to ask questions, like: How might we learn about people and cultures different than our own in a more respectful way? As we seek solutions to environmental problems, how can we ensure that a variety of voices are part of the conversation, including the voices of Native people, many of whom have strong and enduring connections to the land? And how can we study animals without harming them?

These aren't easy questions. But they are exciting questions. They spark innovation. They invite our minds and our hearts to forge new paths. They remind us that the future is ours to imagine—and create.

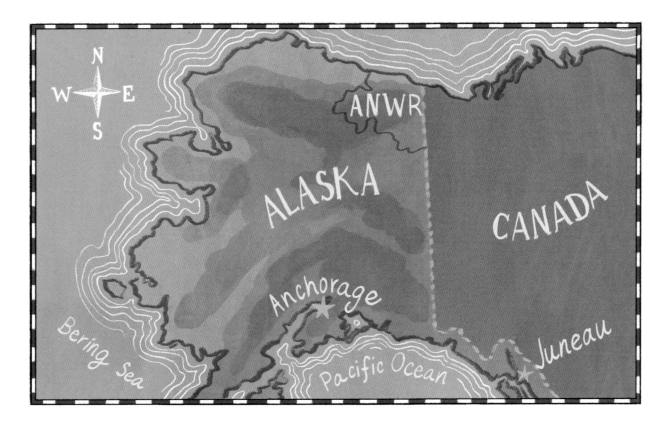

# A Note on Land Conservation ⋘

Our planet's wild places are in danger, more so now than ever before. Even as a new generation of conservationists fights to protect nature, companies continue to cut down forests, drill for oil, and pollute the planet. By burning fossil fuels and releasing harmful chemicals into the air, we are also causing climate change, which is destroying environments and driving animals to extinction.

The creation of national parks and wildlife refuges is one strategy for saving Earth's remaining wilderness—but those parks and refuges have to be constantly defended. Since the Arctic National Wildlife Refuge was created in 1960, oil companies and politicians have tried many times to open up the refuge for drilling. This would hurt the land, the Native people who live there, and countless animals. So far, Alaska Native communities and other environmental activists have been able to keep the refuge safe from drilling, but the fight goes on.

Here are a few organizations devoted to the preservation of wilderness and animals:

- Indigenous Environmental Network
- National Audubon Society
- Sierra Club
- The Nature Conservancy
- Wildlife Conservation Society
- World Wildlife Fund

# A Note on the Native People of Canada and Alaska ⋘

Native people were critical to Olaus and Mardy's ability to navigate and study the North. When Olaus first traveled to Canada to study birds, members of the Ojibwe tribe guided him through the wild and taught him how to canoe properly. He later learned how to travel by sled from the Inuit. During their Arctic travels, the Muries stopped in many Inuit villages, where they were warmly welcomed and given food, directions, and knowledge about animals. Mardy and Olaus's views on nature were shaped by their time with Native people. The beliefs they developed—that nature deserves our respect and that humans are a part of the animal kingdom, not separate from it—have been understood by many Native tribes for time immemorial. In *Journeys to the Far North*, Olaus describes being deeply influenced by the Cree tribe's reverence for nature and animals. Many Native people around the world are leaders of the modern conservation movement. Tribes like the Standing Rock Sioux have been on the frontlines of protesting the construction of harmful oil pipelines, for example, while the Swinomish of the Pacific Northwest released one of the first action plans to address climate change.

## Selected Bibliography ⋘

### Books, Articles, and Essays

Dunlap, Thomas R. "Wildlife, Science, and the National Parks, 1920–1940." *Pacific Historical Review,* vol. 59, no. 2, 1990, pp. 187–202.

Kaye, Roger W. "The Arctic National Wildlife Refuge: An Exploration of the Meanings Embodied in America's Last Great Wilderness." *Wilderness Science in a Time of Change Conference Volume 2: Wilderness Within the Context of Larger Systems.* U.S. Department of Agriculture, Forest Service, 2000, pp. 73–80.

Lawson, Elizabeth. "'What's wrong with a little emotion?' Margaret E. Murie's Wilderness Rhetoric." *Green Voices: Defending Nature and the Environment in American Civic Discourse,* edited by Richard D. Besel and Bernard K. Duffy. State University of New York Press, 2016, pp. 131–152.

Murie, Margaret E. *Two in the Far North, Revised Edition.* Alaska Northwest Books, 2020.

Murie, Olaus J. *Journeys to the Far North, Revised Edition.* Alaska Northwest Books, 2015.

Waterman, Jonathan. *Where the Mountains are Nameless: Passion and Politics in the Arctic National Wildlife.* W.W. Norton & Company, Inc., 2005.

### Congressional Records

United States, Congress, Senate, Committee on Interior and Insular Affairs. *National Wilderness Preservation Act.* U.S. Government Printing Office, 1957. 85th Congress, 1st session.

United States, Congress, Senate, Merchant Marine and Fisheries Subcommittee. *The Arctic Wildlife Range.* U.S. Government Printing Office, 1959. 86th Congress, 1st session.

### Videos and Films

Kreps, Bonnie, producer, writer, and director. *A Superb Naturalist: George Schaller Salutes Olaus Murie.* United States Fish and Wildlife Service.

Kreps, Bonnie, and Craighead, Charles, directors. *Arctic Dance: The Mardy Murie Story.* Bob Swerer Productions, 2001